What I *Love* Most About You™

L

What I *Love* Most About You ™

A KEEPSAKE BOOK FOR THE ONE I TREASURE

wm William Morrow *An Imprint of* HarperCollins*Publishers*

A Redbridge Book

HarperCollins books may be purchased for educational, business, or sales promotional use. For information please write: Special Markets Department, HarperCollins Publishers Inc., 10 East 53rd Street, New York, NY 10022.

FIRST EDITION

Book design by Shubhani Sarkar
Illustrations by Kara Fellows

Printed on acid-free paper

Library of Congress Cataloging-in-Publication Data

Davis, Joann, 1953–
    What I love most about you : a keepsake book for
    the one I treasure.
        p. cm.
    ISBN 0-06-621445-9
    1. Man-woman relationships—Miscellanea.
    2. Love—Miscellanea. I. Title.

    HQ801 .D3428 2002
    306.7—dc21   2001032982

02 03 04 05 06 TWP 10 9 8 7 6 5 4 3 2 1

To:

from:

How do I love thee? Let me count the ways.
I love thee to the depth and breadth and height
my soul can reach. . . .

ELIZABETH BARRETT BROWNING

Introduction

Take a minute, if you will, and ask yourself this question: How often do you tell the special people in your life exactly what it is that you love most about them? How often do you identify what's good about your spouse, lover, children, sisters, brothers, dad, mother, uncles, aunts, friends, and colleagues—and actually put it into words so there can be no doubt? Are you constructive? Do you *celebrate what's good*? Do you extol the ones you love, tell them *how* and *why* you love them in *very specific detail*? Most of us don't take the time to find the good and praise it—or we don't know how.

This little book is designed to change that. Intended to be a token of affection in our busy lives, it's a tool that can promote real intimacy and all its rewards by helping us to *catch our relationships at their best,* to take a snapshot of what is the happiest, most wholesome and wondrous about the special people in our lives. Serving as a prompter, a reminder, this book is also fashioned as a keepsake that will help you put your heart on paper, where it can be seen and shared and felt. In life, our gestures of love go much further if they are indelible, positive, and specific. Our caring should not be left in doubt.

When asked the question, "How do I love thee?" each of us should be ready and able to count the ways.

This book's sentiment is grounded in three secrets of good communication that are at the heart of all relationships:

Communication must be regular
Communication must be constructive
and
Communication must be specific

People in great relationships seem to grasp that life is too short to keep affections locked up or left to the imagination or chance expression.

They know that they must rely heavily on the precious gift that makes human beings so special—the gift of language. They know that positive words are building blocks that help us to foster strong connections and achieve rapport. They understand that when good communication suffers, so do intimacy and closeness, the very special cornerstones of a life worth living. Without these things, without the warmth and the love of the people around us, most of us would feel a gaping hole in our lives.

But creating intimacy doesn't come naturally to everyone. Intimacy takes effort, and it takes time. Sure, there are special occasions when we all testify to what we feel inside—the birthdays and the anniversaries, the holidays and the milestones in life. That's usually when we run out to the card or gift shop because we have permission—or are required—to show that we care. We buy the beautiful bouquet of flowers. Or the box of chocolates. Or we get a greeting card awash in pastel colors and adorned with a poetic inscription. We try to put our affections in a neat prepackaged box with a pretty ribbon and bow.

On many occasions, these thoughtful gestures suffice. (And this little book can serve on those occasions, too!) We are a society of "special occasion" love, and our loved ones know and understand this. But what about the in-between times in life? Or the everyday affections and sentiments? And the most deep-seated feelings we hold in our hearts for the significant people who make up the fabric of our lives? All too often, those important emotions stay bottled up. Our children, our friends, our spouses, our lovers, our family members—we think they know how we feel about them. Often, the very best of what we feel about the close companions who accompany us on our journey through life remains locked inside.

Sometimes it takes a crisis to get out the key or pick the lock. An illness. A calamity. An accident. Or worse. Then, suddenly, the words and the feelings come tumbling out. Imagining life without that person we love makes us remember why we love that person to begin with. If that special person weren't in the equation, what would be lacking? Maybe everything. And do we ever think to say it?

$\mathcal{A}$ relationship counselor with a thriving practice once confided the most effective technique he uses with couples in trouble: At the beginning of every counseling session he asks the quarreling partners to take off their rings (if they wear them) and put them in front of each other. Then the counselor asks each partner to articulate why he or she gave the ring to the other person to begin with. Watching the couples awkwardly shift in their seats, the counselor waits for perfect stillness to settle before going on.

"$\mathcal{S}$o," he states deliberately. "A ring is a powerful symbol of love, a circle of affection for all eternity. What did you see in your partner that made you exchange rings?"

$\mathcal{U}$sually, at this point, you can hear a pin drop. A lot of throat clearing is followed by a lot of soul searching and then, quite often, an avalanche of words spills out—accompanied by tears. The tissues and the handkerchiefs mount up in a heap, along with the dawning recognition that the all-important truth of why they love each other has long gone unspoken, that the light of the truth has dimmed.

"Tell each other," the counselor prompts. "Remind your partner what you love and care about in one another." As the partners recall why the relationship took shape to begin with, the words often become the cement in which the love sets anew.

On the reverse side of the coin are the couples who stay together for decades in continuous bliss. Take the case of the elderly man who was married to the same woman for sixty years. Throughout their years together, without fail, he would regularly come into the kitchen, take his wife into his arms, and dance while singing his own clumsy lyrics to a famous song.

"*The way you wear your bonnet. The way you sip your tea . . . ,*" he would croak in his off-key manner as he spun her around in a dizzying twirl. Sometimes his wife would protest that she was rushing to make dinner or get the dishes cleaned up. But the elderly gentleman would persist. He would occasionally dip her back in a great arch and tell her what he loved most about her, each time adding something new and tenderhearted.

"*I* love the way you make spaghetti sauce," he would say, then add, "and I love the way you tie your hair back in a great knot. I love the cookies you make for the grandchildren and how you pretend not to notice when I sneak a few before the kids arrive. I love your bright red lipstick—it's a shade the young women don't wear anymore. I love the way you concentrate on your needlepoint in your easy chair each night. I love the pillow covers that you make—they remind me of you wherever I sit."

Although her back was often sore because they dipped too often, the wife knew how her husband felt about her. He was reaffirming his love for his lifetime partner in very specific ways. There wasn't another person on earth who could have said the same things quite the same way. And all who knew the couple attributed the longevity of their years to the way they conveyed their affections fully and completely. They expressed themselves. There was never any doubt.

To express. To leave no doubt. Very simply put, communication leaves no doubt. To hold out what we hold most dear. To acknowledge in all of its glory what is special. To showcase the inside on the outside. At the heart of every vibrant relationship is an ability to do that.

What, then, do we want to acknowledge in those we love?

If they possess a specific virtue, quality, characteristic, idiosyncrasy, or unique talent, tell them. Don't assume they know. It could be something outward—style, clothing, wardrobe, dress. It could be qualities of the inner or outer self. Personality traits. Manners. The points that make them who they are. Their character traits and quirks. Tell them. Don't assume they know. And then, when you have told them, stand back and watch what happens. Often there is a blossoming. Sometimes the results are miraculous as people who are close grow closer. Love begins to radiate out.

As you read through the 401 entries that follow in the pages of *What I Love Most About You,* keep that special person to whom you are giving this book in your heart and in your soul. As you survey the qualities we have gathered together to help you celebrate the one you hold so dear, put a little asterisk or draw a tiny heart beside each entry you feel best illustrates what makes him or her so special to you.

And because each person is unique, you might also want to list some observations that are all your own. That's why we have left space, so that you can make this a very personal celebration of the one you love. Don't hesitate to say something personal. This is your time and your chance. Find the good in the one you love—and praise it!

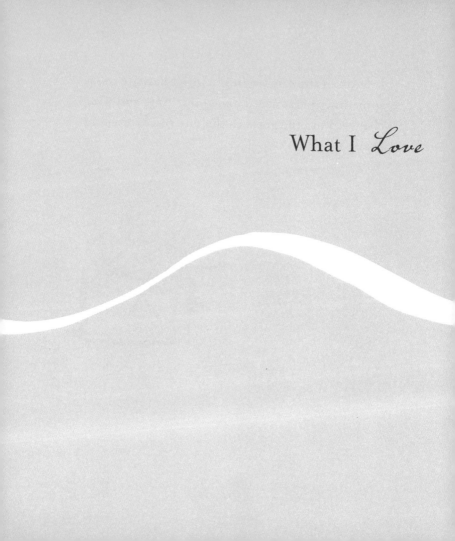

What I *Love*

Most About You

( ) *I love* your smile.

( ) *I love* the way you cover your eyes
during the scary parts at the movies.

( ) *I love* your gentle nature.

( ) *I love* how you brighten up my life.

*"The love we give away is
the only love we keep."*
ELBERT HUBBERT

( ) *I love* your indomitable spirit.

( ) *I love* how you sing off-key in
the shower.

( ) *I love* how you give me your full
attention when we talk.

( ) *I love* your willingness to help
me in any way possible when I
have a problem.

( ) *I love* how your hair looks when you've just had it cut.

( ) *I love* your single-mindedness.

( ) *I love* how you look when you wake up in the morning.

( ) *I love* your handwriting.

( ) *I love* that you always rise to the occasion.

( ) *I love* your strong character.

( ) *I love* your ability to forgive and really forget.

( ) *I love* how cuddly you are.

( ) *I love* how you try to make peace whenever there is a conflict.

( ) *I love* how you always look for common ground when it would be so easy to argue.

( ) *I love* the courage you show in times of adversity.

( ) *I love* your fierce sense of determination.

( ) *I love* your strong sense of fair play.

( ) *I love* the value you place on truth.

( ) *I love* the value you place on justice.

( ) *I love* how free you make me feel to tell you the absolute truth.

( ) *I love* how safe I feel whenever I am
with you.

( ) *I love* your strong sense of loyalty.

( ) *I love* how you get down on the floor and
wrestle whenever there are children around
to play with.

( ) *I love* the value you place on faith.

*"The manner of giving
is worth more than
the gift."*
PIERRE CORNEILLE

(21)

*"You learn to love
by loving."*
ALDOUS HUXLEY

( ) *I love* the value you place on friendship.

( ) *I love* how you always emphasize the
positive.

( ) *I love* how you give me breathing space
when I need it most.

( ) *I love* the value you place on family.

( ) *I love* your ability to let
loose and have a good time.

( ) *I love* how you always
take time to think before you speak.

( ) *I love* how you think on
your feet.

( ) *I love* your sense of delicacy.

(23)

( ) *I love* your natural poise.

( ) *I love* how strongly you defend
your deeply held beliefs.

( ) *I love* the tolerance you show to
others with different points of view.

( ) *I love* sharing popcorn with you
at the movies.

( ) *I love* how you snuggle under
the blankets in bed on a cold night.

( ) *I love* your outgoing personality.

( ) *I love* your calm temperament.

( ) *I love* how you get really passionate
discussing politics.

*"Love isn't love till you
give it away."*
OSCAR HAMMERSTEIN

(25)

( ) *I love* your fiery temperament.

( ) *I love* the quietude that follows
you wherever you go.

( ) *I love* your rugged
individualism.

( ) *I love* your
bold sense of
adventure.

( ) *I love* your contagious high-energy level.

( ) *I love* your infectious laugh.

( ) *I love* how you're always ready
to send flowers, no matter
the occasion.

( ) *I love* your levelheadedness.

( ) *I love* how you always check up on
your relatives.

( ) *I love* how you roll up your sleeves
and help without being asked.

( ) *I love* your down-to-earth nature.

( ) *I love* your unerring good judgment.

> *"Where there is great
> love, there are always
> miracles."*
> WILLA CATHER

(28)

( ) *I love* your sense of discipline.

( ) *I love* your sense of patriotism.

( ) *I love* your love
of learning.

( ) *I love* your high IQ.

( ) *I love* your willingness to defend what you think is right, even against fierce opposition.

( ) *I love* how clean and scrubbed you always look after showering.

( ) *I love* your sense of style.

( ) *I love* your incredible charisma.

( ) *I love* the way you light up any room
you enter.

( ) *I love* how you look when you wear red.

( ) *I love* how you look when you wear black.

( ) *I love* how you look when you wear yellow.

"Love doesn't make the
world go 'round. Love is
what makes the ride
worthwhile."
FRANKLIN P. JONES

(31)

( ) *I love* how you look when you wear blue.

( ) *I love* how you look when you wear purple.

( ) *I love* how you look when you wear pink.

( ) *I love* that you can make me laugh even when I'm mad at you.

( ) *I love* your willingness to
live and let live.

( ) *I love* your unwillingness
to tolerate prejudice.

( ) *I love* how you can stay
up all night just talking
to me.

( ) *I love* your sense of
social activism.

> *"Acts of love enkindle and
> melt the soul."*
> ST. TERESA OF AVILA

( ) *I love* your dedication to self-
improvement.

( ) *I love* how you always look on
the bright side of every situation.

( ) *I love* your extraordinary willpower.

( ) *I love* your creativity.

( ) *I love* your efficiency, how you get
the job done.

( ) *I love* your punctuality.

( ) *I love* how mischievous you are.

( ) *I love* how you cheat at cards when you
think I'm not looking.

( ) *I love* your joie de vivre.

( ) *I love* how you luxuriate in the bathtub.

( ) *I love* your ability to take time out,
to relax.

( ) *I love* when you throw a meal
together—or just order in.

> *"To cheat oneself out of
> love is the most terrible
> deception; it is an eternal
> loss for which there is no
> reparation, either in time
> or in eternity."*
> KIERKEGAARD

( ) *I love* your love of books
and ideas.

( ) *I love* the good care
you take of your body.

( ) *I love* your ability
to pick up other
languages.

( ) *I love* that you spend whole weekends
curled up in bed with a good book.

"Two humans make one love divine."
ELIZABETH BARRETT
BROWNING

( ) *I love* the way you support and encourage others around you.

( ) *I love* that you express outrage when somebody is treated unfairly.

( ) *I love* your leadership skills.

( ) *I love* your natural ability to take charge.

( ) *I love* your love of sports.

( ) *I love* your taste in clothes.

( ) *I love* your athleticism.

( ) *I love* how you always play to win.

( ) *I love* your desire to be a "team player."

( ) *I love* how you try, in everything you do,
to give it your all.

( ) *I love* the way you play with your dogs.

( ) *I love* the way you adore your cats.

( ) *I love* the way you treat animals with care and kindness.

( ) *I love* your fearless ability to stand up against the crowd.

( ) *I love* your deep sense of humility.

( ) *I love* your selflessness.

( ) *I love* how you can always be
differentiated in a crowd,
how you cut a unique profile.

( ) *I love* your gregarious nature.

( ) *I love* your civic-mindedness.

( ) *I love* your charitable nature.

*"Love is that condition in
which the happiness of
another person is essential
to your own."*
ROBERT A. HEINLEIN

( ) *I love* how thick-skinned you are.

( ) *I love* how water rolls off your back.

( ) *I love* how tenacious you are.

( ) *I love* how you tuck me into bed when you
have to work late.

( ) *I love* your ability to have fun in a
childlike way.

( ) *I love* how unsinkable you are, even
when trouble is brewing.

( ) *I love* your impeccable sense of timing,
how you call or show up at the right
moment.

( ) *I love* your intuitive nature.

( ) *I love* how tuned in you are to what's important at all times.

( ) *I love* that you feel things deeply.

( ) *I love* your profound sense of idealism.

( ) *I love* your optimism.

"Love is what you've been through with somebody."
JAMES THURBER

( ) *I love* your realism.

( ) *I love* how you always step up and are
"the grown-up" in situations where one
is needed.

( ) *I love* your appreciation of nature
and the outdoors.

( ) *I love* your appreciation
for flowers of all kinds
and colors.

(46)

( ) *I love* how you carry on a conversation.

( ) *I love* your commitment to the environment.

( ) *I love* your facility with words, you're such a word person.

( ) *I love* your ability to do the crossword puzzle quickly—and in ink.

"If one wishes to be a lover, he must start by saying 'Yes' to love."
LEO BUSCAGLIA

( ) *I love* how dependable you are.

( ) *I love* how you get silly.

( ) *I love* how you giggle.

( ) *I love* when you get hysterical and can't stop laughing.

(48)

( ) *I love* how your face gets beet red when you're embarrassed.

( ) *I love* how you hold babies with tenderness and care.

( ) *I love* how you always put others first.

( ) *I love* how you always show respect for all people, no matter who they are.

( ) *I love* how you value the simple things.

( ) *I love* just knowing you are there.

( ) *I love* your taste in music.

( ) *I love* your taste in art.

"Through love, through friendship, a heart lives more than one life."
ANAÏS NIN

( ) *I love* the way you get lost in works of art.

( ) *I love* just hanging out with you,
doing nothing.

( ) *I love* having any kind
of fun with you because
you intensify it.

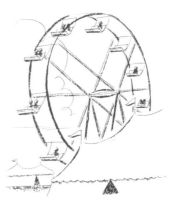

( ) *I love* your love of
amusement parks.

( ) *I love* when you get frisky like a
puppy and just want to play and laugh.

( ) *I love* your supreme confidence
in yourself.

( ) *I love* the confidence you place in me.

( ) *I love* being by your side.

*"If I speak in human and
angelic tongues, but do
not have love, I am a
resounding gong or a
clashing cymbal."*
1 CORINTHIANS

( ) *I love* how you whisper in my ear
at parties.

( ) *I love* the sound of your voice.

( ) *I love* holding
your hand.

( ) *I love* getting
a small note or
letter from you.

( ) *I love* the little ways you always stay in touch, no matter how far away you are from me.

( ) *I love* how you always know when I need you.

( ) *I love* knowing I can count on you.

( ) *I love* how you're up at midnight to check on the children.

> *"It is not only necessary to love, it is necessary to say so."*
> FRENCH PROVERB

( ) *I love* knowing you will stand by me, no matter what.

( ) *I love* the way you treat older people.

( ) *I love* the way you look after your mother.

( ) *I love* the way you look after your father.

( ) *I love* the way you look after your brothers.

( ) *I love* the way you look after your sisters.

( ) *I love* that you tell me stories about you as a kid.

( ) *I love* how you always stop to ask if you can help the elderly cross the street.

( ) *I love* how you always pass along items you've clipped out of the paper that you think will interest me.

( ) *I love* your sense of responsibility.

( ) *I love* the color of your skin.

( ) *I love* your spontaneity.

"If you can learn from hard knocks, you can also learn from soft touches."
CAROLYN KENMORE

(57)

"Love is not blind, it sees more, not less. But because it sees more, it is willing to see less."

RABBI JULIUS GORDON

( ) *I love* your sense of devotion.

( ) *I love* your spirituality.

( ) *I love* your unshakable belief in God.

( ) *I love* the trust you put in prayer.

( ) *I love* your intensity.

( ) *I love* how you attack a problem.

( ) *I love* how you believe any problem
can be solved.

( ) *I love* the way you crush me when
you hug me.

( ) *I love* your soft, tender embrace.

( ) *I love* how you push me to do things I wouldn't normally do.

( ) *I love* that you always read our horoscopes out loud.

( ) *I love* your belief in the idea that "nice guys finish first."

> *"There is no remedy for love but to love more."*
> HENRY DAVID THOREAU

( ) *I love* your ability to negotiate a sticky situation.

( ) *I love* how you tiptoe around when you think I am asleep.

( ) *I love* your thoughtfulness.

( ) *I love* that you always let me have the last piece of pie.

*"To love and be loved
is to feel the sun from
both sides."*
DAVID VISCOTT

( ) *I love* how traditional you are.

( ) *I love* how sentimental you are.

( ) *I love* the value you put on family time.

( ) *I love* the value you put on rituals.

( ) *I love* the value you place on downtime.

( ) *I love* that you know how important it is to get away.

( ) *I love* how you live your life in order to avoid the rat race.

( ) *I love* your old-fashioned approach to life.

( ) *I love* your sense
of chivalry.

( ) *I love* your sense of honor.

( ) *I love* the way you treat a lady.

( ) *I love* your unfailing sense of politeness.

"Those who bring sunshine into the lives of others cannot keep it from themselves."

SIR JAMES BARRIE

( ) *I love* your playfulness.

( ) *I love* your dedication to your work.

( ) *I love* your quick wit.

( ) *I love* how affectionate you are.

( ) *I love* your sense of decorum.

( ) *I love* how well you adapt to your
surroundings.

( ) *I love* your sense of generosity.

( ) *I love* how at home you are with yourself.

*"Love begins when a person
feels another person's
need to be as important
as his own."*
HENRY STACK SULLIVAN

(66)

( ) *I love* that you're always up for hearing
some juicy gossip.

( ) *I love* the way you hold me in the night.

( ) *I love* how you always think of others'
feelings.

( ) *I love* the way you cook.

( ) *I love* that you've
taught me how to
appreciate wine.

( ) *I love* how
organized you are.

( ) *I love* how you
keep your priorities straight.

( ) *I love* that you always do the unexpected.

( ) *I love* how you put people at ease.

( ) *I love* that you never lose your cool.

( ) *I love* that you can never decide which
shoes to wear.

( ) *I love* how you work to make your
dreams—and mine—a reality.

( ) *I love* how you "seize the day."

( ) *I love* how we fit together like two pieces of a puzzle.

( ) *I love* the way you do the things you do.

( ) *I love* how you savor every new experience and challenge.

"I love you so passionately,
that I hide a great part
of my love, not to
oppress you with it."
MARIE DE RABUTIN-
CHANTAL

( ) *I love* how you love to try new foods.

( ) *I love* how you love to travel to new places.

( ) *I love* how you keep meticulous records of the important events in your life.

( ) *I love* how you avoid what is trivial and attract what is essential.

( ) *I love* your sense of awe and wonder
at the universe.

( ) *I love* how you always
wish on the first
star in the night sky.

( ) *I love* the way you
care for your
houseplants as if they
were roommates.

( ) *I love* drinking hot
chocolate with you when it's cold outside.

( ) *I love* your sense of decency.

( ) *I love* your willingness to gamble, to go for broke, if your gut tells you to.

( ) *I love* how in touch you are with yourself.

( ) *I love* how you stay true to your beliefs.

"If I have all faith so as to move mountains but do not have love, I am nothing."
1 CORINTHIANS

( ) *I love* how you want to see the entire world—and take me with you.

( ) *I love* how you practice what you preach.

( ) *I love* that you believe in "When in Rome" and try out all the customs of the place we're visiting.

( ) *I love* rolling in the crisp autumn leaves with you.

( ) *I love* watching the sunrise with you.

( ) *I love* watching the sun set with you.

( ) *I love* driving in the country with you.

( ) *I love* going shopping with you.

( ) *I love* sharing an "in" joke with you.

( ) *I love* when you sing along with the radio when you don't know the words.

( ) *I love* the little things you do to show that you care—bring flowers, light candles.

( ) *I love* how you touch me.

"Till I loved I never lived."
EMILY DICKINSON

( ) *I love* dancing up a storm with you.

( ) *I love* going out and staying out until dawn with you.

( ) *I love* how you tear into your birthday presents with wild enthusiasm.

( ) *I love* how you recap an entire game for me.

( ) *I love* how you brush your hair from your face.

( ) *I love* your firm sense of purpose.

( ) *I love* how you always strive to reach your potential.

( ) *I love* that you long to create meaning in your life.

( ) *I love* the value you put on community.

( ) *I love* how you always see the beauty in everything.

( ) *I love* how you stamp out negative thinking.

( ) *I love* that you're always willing to change channels and watch what I want.

( ) *I love* how elegant you are.

( ) *I love* what a sucker you are for silly puns.

( ) *I love* how you sneak into the kitchen for
a snack when you think nobody's looking.

( ) *I love* your firm backbone.

( ) *I love* how you hold your ground when
you are right.

( ) *I love* how you compromise when
you decide it is most effective.

( ) *I love* your firm moral values.

( ) *I love* your sense of mercy.

*"They do not love that do
not show their love."*
WILLIAM SHAKESPEARE

( ) *I love* your sense of goodness.

( ) *I love* your sense of grace.

( ) *I love* your unwillingness to compromise when principle is at stake.

( ) *I love* how you automatically get up to dance when you hear a song you love.

( ) *I love* how you eat with gusto.

( ) *I love* how you eat like a pig and still manage to stay thin.

( ) *I love* how you practice random acts of kindness.

( ) *I love* how you never have a bad word to say about anybody.

( ) *I love* how soft your skin is.

( ) *I love* how you don't take others for granted.

( ) *I love* how we've grown together through the years.

( ) *I love* how you treasure our memories together.

( ) *I love* your wrinkled skin.

( ) *I love* how careworn your face is.

( ) *I love* how you always stop to smell the flowers—and make me breathe them in, too.

( ) *I love* how you burst with pride when something good happens to a friend.

"Whatever our souls are made of, his and mine are the same."
EMILY BRONTË

( ) *I love* your intense work ethic.

( ) *I love* the attitude you display in the face of adversity.

( ) *I love* how you tuck your warm feet under mine in the early morning hours.

( ) *I love* the way you revel at the rain.

> *"Ah! Life grows lovely*
> *where you are."*
> MATHILDE BLIND

( ) *I love* how you look when you are dressed to the nines.

( ) *I love* the way you pretend that you are watching the movie when I know that you are dozing off.

( ) *I love* that you want to teach me everything.

( ) *I love* how you say, "It's only money," when a loss has been suffered.

(87)

"Love is a game where two can play and both can win."
EVA GABOR

( ) *I love* your willingness to share everything with me.

( ) *I love* your willingness to do the dishes and to help around the house.

( ) *I love* how you get pumped up when your team is winning.

( ) *I love* how you keep rooting for your team even when they are down.

(88)

( ) *I love* that you can quote from movies.

( ) *I love* how you share your deepest
feelings, even when you are disappointed
in yourself.

( ) *I love* your strong belief that everyone
should give back to the world.

( ) *I love* how you get so happy it's like
a reflex.

( ) *I love* the way you read me special passages
from books you think I might enjoy.

( ) *I love* how you
bring me tea and
soup and toast
when I am sick.

( ) *I love* how you
hold me when
something makes
me cry.

( ) *I love* how you always say "thank you" and
show your gratitude.

( ) *I love* how you can build or fix anything.

( ) *I love* how aware you always stay of
current events.

( ) *I love* your wild streak.

( ) *I love* your knowledge of history.

( ) *I love* that you are a math person.

( ) *I love* that you are a computer whiz.

( ) *I love* how you always keep your emotions in check.

( ) *I love* the way you make a pancake breakfast on the weekend.

> *"You can give without*
> *loving but you can't love*
> *without giving."*
> AMY CARMICHAEL

( ) *I love* how you can get annoyed one
minute and put the problem aside the next.

( ) *I love* the way you can talk things out.

( ) *I love* the way you don't hold a grudge.

( ) *I love* the way you turn any gathering into
a party.

> *"No one has ever measured,
> even the poets, how much
> a heart can hold."*
> ZELDA FITZGERALD

( ) *I love* that I feel sparks whenever I'm
near you.

( ) *I love* that you call in sick for me so we can
spend the day together.

( ) *I love* the way you give a massage.

( ) *I love* your ability to console people
when they are sad.

( ) *I love* how you save
your money for a
rainy day.

( ) *I love* how you make sure
everyone is provided for around
the holidays.

( ) *I love* how you generate new ideas
in any situation.

( ) *I love* how cerebral you are.

(95)

( ) *I love* your piercing blue eyes.

( ) *I love* your perfect green eyes.

( ) *I love* your deep brown eyes.

( ) *I love* your moody hazel eyes.

( ) *I love* your dimples.

( ) *I love* the child
within you that often
comes out.

( ) *I love* how you
always try to do what
is right.

( ) *I love* that you are flexible and make
changes when they are necessary.

( ) *I love* that you never pretend to be something you are not.

( ) *I love* your sense of modesty.

( ) *I love* that you brag about your family and take pride in everyone's accomplishments.

( ) *I love* that you believe in angels.

> "The greatest happiness in life is the conviction that we are loved, loved for ourselves, or rather, loved in spite of ourselves."
> VICTOR HUGO

( ) *I love* how you love to analyze movies.

( ) *I love* that you make every day different
from the one before.

( ) *I love* that you take pleasure in surprising
people.

( ) *I love* that you sometimes call me just
to say "hi."

( ) *I love* how you look when you
are just wearing an old pair of jeans
and a sweater.

( ) *I love* how expressive your face is.

( ) *I love* that you make no demands
on me.

( ) *I love* that your love is always
unconditional.

( ) *I love* that you never break your promises.

( ) *I love* how you use your hands when
you talk.

( ) *I love* your expressive body language.

( ) *I love* the way your eyes twinkle.

*"Every time you think
positive thoughts, you
grow in love."*
ANONYMOUS

( ) *I love* that you scream on roller coasters.

( ) *I love* the fact that you are a collector
and take pride in your special hobbies.

( ) *I love* your profile.

( ) *I love* that you are a movie buff.

( ) *I love* how you have helped me become more loving by setting such a wonderful example.

( ) *I love* how you're always ready, camera in hand, to record every moment.

( ) *I love* that you are never hasty.

( ) *I love* that you know when to be patient and when to act.

"When love reigns,
the impossible may
be attained."
INDIAN PROVERB

( ) *I love* how sensitive you are to light
and color.

( ) *I love* how you appreciate a rainbow.

( ) *I love* your incredible sense of direction.

( ) *I love* how
charming and
debonair you are.

( ) *I love* that you can sew.

( ) *I love* that you can always pick out
the perfect gift for a friend.

( ) *I love* how you always call me when
the weather is bad and I have to travel,
telling me to be careful.

( ) *I love* how you tuck the children in bed
at night with tender loving care.

( ) *I love* your ability to
always be pleasant in
any situation.

( ) *I love* how you love
to throw snowballs
and have fun when
the flakes fly.

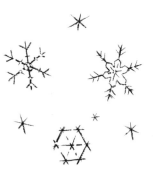

( ) *I love* how you gently blow
on the children's skinned knees when
they fall and try to kiss the hurt away.

( ) *I love* that you accept my quirks.

( ) *I love* that you sit and veg with me in front of the TV.

( ) *I love* your love of drama.

( ) *I love* your love of museums.

( ) *I love* your love of architecture and how you comment on buildings.

( ) *I love* your love of technical things.

( ) *I love* how you ramble when you're
nervous.

( ) *I love* how you're my cheerleader in
all things.

( ) *I love* when you say, "Come sit and
tell me about it."

*"The best gifts are tied
with heart strings."*
ANONYMOUS

( ) *I love* that you value my time.

( ) *I love* that you always make time
for friends—both yours and mine.

( ) *I love* that you can occupy yourself.

( ) *I love* that you can sit by the water and
fish all day.

( ) *I love* how you honor your vows.

( ) *I love* that you know when to quit.

( ) *I love* that you never push me to
my limits.

( ) *I love* that you know
when to be self-sufficient
and when to ask for help.

( ) *I love* your love of handmade things.

( ) *I love* that you are not materialistic.

( ) *I love* your pin-straight hair.

( ) *I love* your wild, curly hair.

( ) *I love* your fiery red hair.

( ) *I love* your jet-black hair.

( ) *I love* your auburn hair.

( ) *I love* your luxurious blond hair.

( ) *I love* your wavy hair.

( ) *I love* your hair when you let it grow long.

( ) *I love* your hair when you keep it cropped short.

( ) *I love* that you are still a wonder to me after all this time.

( ) *I love* that I knew you were the one from the first moment I saw you.

( ) *I love* that you keep me to yourself.

( ) *I love* to love you.

( ) *I love* the way you love me.

( ) *I love* you I love you I do!

What I *Love* Most About You

Below is space to make note of other very special qualities.

_____

_____

_____

_____

_____

_____

_____

_____

_____

_____

_____

_____

_____

finis